The Kings Of England

THE KINGS OF ENGLAND;

ARRANGED AND ILLUSTRATED

FOR THE YOUNG.

NEW YORK:
PUBLISHED BY JOSIAH ADAMS,
BRICK CHURCH CHAPEL, NEAR THE CITY HALL.

1845.

[Entered according to Act of Congress, in the year 1844, by JOSIAH ADAMS, in the Clerk's Office of the District Court of the Southern District of New York.]

STEREOTYPED BY T. B. SMITH,
216 WILLIAM STREET, NEW YORK.

CONTENTS.

	Page
PREFACE	5
EARLY HISTORY	7
WILLIAM I.	17
WILLIAM II.	21
HENRY I.	25
STEPHEN	29
HENRY II.	33
RICHARD I.	39
JOHN	43
HENRY III.	47
EDWARD I.	51
EDWARD II.	55
EDWARD III.	59
RICHARD II.	63
HENRY IV.	67
HENRY V.	71
HENRY VI.	75
EDWARD IV.	79
EDWARD V.	83
RICHARD III.	87
HENRY VII.	91
HENRY VIII.	95
EDWARD VI.	99
MARY	103

CONTENTS.

	PAGE
ELIZABETH	107
JAMES I.	111
CHARLES I.	115
CROMWELL	119
CHARLES II.	123
JAMES II.	127
WILLIAM AND MARY	131
ANNE	135
GEORGE I.	139
GEORGE II.	143
GEORGE III.	147
GEORGE IV.	151
WILLIAM IV.	155
VICTORIA	159
REGAL SUCCESSION	161

PREFACE.

This little book, suggested by "THE GAME OF KINGS," and in part composed of the same materials, is designed to aid the young learner in the effort to fix in his memory the dates of some of the principal events in the History of England. It is, of course, a mere epitome. But it is hoped that the incidents are so arranged and illustrated as to engage the attention and amuse the mind of the young, and thus facilitate the acquisition of that kind of knowledge, which, in itself, is dry and unattractive. The Book will be found an agreeable accompaniment to "THE GAME OF KINGS."

THE KINGS OF ENGLAND.

EARLY HISTORY.

The early history of England is involved in great obscurity. All that is known of it, down to the eighth or ninth century after Christ, may be written in a few brief pages.

Fifty-five years before Christ, Julius Cæsar, the great Roman general, thinking that all the world ought to belong to Rome, went over to England, to conquer it. He met with little success, however, and soon returned, leaving only a garrison behind him. About one hundred years after, in the year 43, Aulus Plautius, another Roman general, was sent, with a large army, to England, and in the year 60, Suetonius completed the conquest, and made the Island a Roman Colony. The northern part of it, however, then called Caledonia, now Scotland, they could never subdue.

The religion of the Britons was a terrible superstition. They were governed by priests, who were called Druids, who offered human sacrifices to their gods. The conquest of the Romans was a great blessing to the island, for it destroyed the Druids, and introduced the christian religion, and the arts of civilization. St. Paul, in his missionary journeyings is supposed to have travelled as far as England, where he preached Christ to the people, and laid the foundation of a church.

The Romans kept possession of England till about 414, when their Governors and soldiers were all recalled and the Britons left to themselves.

When the Romans were gone, the unconquered Scots, from the mountains of Caledonia, came down upon the Britons, and made dreadful havoc among them. They sent to beg assistance from Rome; but Rome was then too weak to help them. They then asked aid from the Saxons, who dwelt in the northern part of Germany.

The Saxons came over about 460, with an army under Hengist and Horsa, two brothers, and soon drove the Scots back to their mountains. But they liked the country so well, that they concluded to stay there; so they turned their arms upon the poor Britons, and subdued them. Horsa was killed in battle, and Hengist made himself king of a part of the island called Kent.

After this, other Saxons came over in great numbers, and got possession of all Britain; dividing it into seven kingdoms, called the Saxon Heptarchy. One of these kingdoms was called Anglia—from this the whole country began to be called Angleland, and afterwards England. Of the poor Britons but few were left. The whole country was overrun with Saxons, except Cambria, now called Wales, which the remnant kept possession of till 1300, when it was conquered by Edward I.

The Saxon conquest drove out the christian religion, and established pagan worship again in England. The Britons in Wales, however, still held fast to the christian faith ; and when, about a century afterwards, the Roman catholic missionaries went there, they found them believers in Christ. In the sixth century, the whole country was converted to christianity.

But little is known of the Heptarchy, or of any of the kings of this period. Sebert, one of the kings of Essex, is said to have founded Westminster Abbey, in the year 600, which still remains, though with many additions, one of the wonders of England.

In the year 827, Egbert, King of Wessex, completed the conquest of the seven kingdoms, and reduced them to one, under the name of England. Ireland was added in 1172, under Henry II. Wales in 1300, by Edward I, and Scotland in 1602, by James I., who was heir to both kingdoms.

Egbert and his successors, of the Saxon race, continued to reign over England, nearly two hundred years, when the Danes, after several invasions, and many years of cruel war, conquered the country, and made Canute king, in 1016. The throne was recovered by the Saxons, under Edward the Confessor, in 1041, but lost again, by the invasion of the Normans under William the Conqueror, in 1066. The Normans reigned nearly one hundred years, when the Saxon line was again restored by Henry II. in 1154. Since then, the Saxons, or

Anglo-Saxons, as they are generally called, have been undisputed masters of the soil and throne of England.

SAXONS.

827.	Egbert,	9
836.	Ethelwolf,	21
857.	Ethelred I.	14
871.	ALFRED, (Oxford University,)	30
901.	Edward, the Elder, (Cambridge University,)	24
925.	Athelston,	16
941.	Edmund,	7
948.	Ederd,	7
955.	Edwy,	4
959.	Edgar,	16
975.	Edward, the Martyr,	4
979.	Ethelred II.	37
1016.	Edmund, Ironsides,	1

DANES.

1017.	Canute,	18
1035.	Harold, Harefoot,	4
1039.	Hardicanute,	2

SAXONS.

1041.	Edward, the Confessor,	25
1066.	Harold, Earl Godwin,	

Of the early Saxon kings, we know but little that can be depended upon. The most distinguished among them, was Alfred the Great, whose reign commenced in 871. At twelve years of age, he had not been taught to read. But about this time, hearing his mother sing some Saxon poems, he was seized with a great desire to learn. He applied himself so diligently, that he was soon able to read, not only in Saxon, but in Latin. He was a great lover of learning, and one of the best examples of royalty recorded in any History. He laid the foundation of the University at Oxford, and established schools in all parts of his kingdom.

ALFRED AND HIS MOTHER.

An interesting story is told of Alfred taking refuge in the house of a peasant. The Danes had been troublesome neighbors to the English, for some years. Soon after Alfred came to the throne, they came over in large numbers, and Alfred loving peace more than war, gave them money to quit the country. This only brought over larger numbers, and they finally drove him from his throne, and for some time he wandered about, in solitary places, till at last he found a place of refuge in the cottage of a swine-herd. He was in disguise, and the cottager did not know who he was. Alfred, while there endeavored to make himself useful, and undertook one day to watch the good woman's cakes, while she went to attend to her other affairs. But the poor king was so much engrossed with the desperate affairs of the kingdom, that he forgot to look after the cakes, so that they were so sadly burned, that they were not fit to be eaten. The woman scolded him severely, on her return, taunting him with being willing to eat of her bread, while he would not even take the trouble to turn it, to save it from being spoiled. He took the reproof very kindly, and promised to do better, if she should try him again. She did so, and he baked the cakes to her entire satisfaction.

ALFRED DISGUISED AS A HARPER.

Soon after this he gathered some of his friends around him, and made preparations to attack the Danes. He first, in the disguise of a harper, visited their camp, and ascertained that they were not so powerful as he had supposed, and then, attacking them suddenly, defeated them. He did not destroy them, but made them friends, by giving them lands, and encouraging them to be good citizens.

EARLY HISTORY. 13

Oi the Danish kings, there were only three. The first was Canute, sometimes called Canute the Great, because he was king of Denmark and Norway, as well as of England.

At one time when worshipping in the Cathedral at Winchester, he took off his crown and hung it on the cross, and could never afterwards be prevailed on to wear it.

CANUTE THE GREAT ON THE SEA SHORE

Sitting one day on the sea shore, his courtiers flattered him, by telling him that he was all powerful, and that nothing could resist him. The tide was fast coming in, and every wave approached nearer to his seat. At last it washed over his feet. "Thou art under my dominion," said he to the ocean, "this is my land, approach no farther, nor dare to wet thy sovereign's feet." The next wave dashed over him, when looking sternly at his flatterers, he rebuked them, for giving honor to him, which belongs to God alone.

2

WILLIAM I.

FIRST NORMAN.

1066.

WILLIAM THE CONQUEROR.

William, duke of Normandy, claimed the throne of England, under the pretence that Edward the Confessor had left it to him in his will. He came over, with an army; and on the 14th of October, 1066, in the battle of Hastings, was completely victorious. He was crowned at Westminster, on Christmas day.

Edgar Atheling was the true heir to the throne, and William paid him a mark a day, to renounce his pretensions. A mark is nearly equal to three crowns.

William's sons, Robert and William, were very quarrelsome, and turbulent. Robert proceeded to open rebellion against his father, and meeting him in battle, was near killing him. The king called out, and Robert, knowing his voice, sprung from his horse, in an agony of grief, threw himself on his knees, and begged his father's forgiveness. William was too much incensed to forgive him at once; but afterwards his queen Matilda prevailed on him to pardon his son.

After this, William made war against France. He was very cruel, burning every thing as he went.

His cruelty brought its own punishment; for, after burning the town of Mantes, his horse, flinching from the smoke, made a violent plunge, which threw the king forward upon the saddle-bow; and being very corpulent, he received a bruise, which caused his death.

William planted the "New Forest" in Hampshire, for a hunting ground, destroying thirty villages, and driving out the inhabitants, to make room for it.

He also caused the "Dooms-day Book" to be made, containing a survey of the whole kingdom, with the extent of every parish, and all the particulars respecting it. This is still preserved in the Tower.

William tried to introduce the French language, instead of the Saxon, but did not succeed. He ordered that nothing but French or Latin should be taught in the schools. But yet it is curious to find how much more of the Saxon there is in our language, than of the French. For instance, out of sixty-nine words, which make up the Lord's prayer, there are only five which are not Saxon.

WILLIAM II.

SECOND NORMAN.

1087.

WILLIAM RUFUS.

WILLIAM II. was called Rufus, because his complexion was ruddy, and his hair red. He was a low, vulgar, passionate man. His brother Robert was duke of Normandy. The English preferred him to William, and tried to make him king; but without success. And Robert's attention was soon diverted from it, by a great zeal for the Crusades, or Holy Wars. These were wars, in which nearly all the Christian nations were engaged, for the conquest of Jerusalem. They thought that the place where Christ was buried ought not to be in the hands of infidels, or Mahometans; so they sent large armies to conquer the Holy Land, and many hundred thousands lost their lives in these wars, without gaining any permanent advantage.

The Crusaders were very ardent in the cause, and they wore a red cross on their shoulders, as a sign, or badge. Robert, duke of Normandy, was so eager to engage in this war, that he mortgaged his crown to his brother William, for ten thousand marks, in order to pay the expense.

William took possession of Normandy, but did not long enjoy his bargain. While hunting in the

New Forest, a gentleman, named Walter Tyrrell, shot an arrow at a deer. The arrow struck the bough of a tree, which changed its direction, and it pierced the heart of the king, who fell dead on the spot.

His character was such that he was not lamented by the people. They did not even pay a common respect to his remains; but suffered his body to lie unnoticed in the forest, where it fell. After a while, it was taken up by some poor peasants living near, and buried.

HENRY I.

THIRD NORMAN.

1100.

HENRY BEAUCLERC.

When William Rufus was killed, his brother Henry, surnamed Beauclerc, because he was a good scholar, seized all his treasures, and persuaded the people to proclaim him king, though Robert, being older, was entitled to the crown. But Robert was absent, on a crusade. When he returned, he took possession of Normandy, and made an effort to conquer his brother Henry. But Henry afterwards made Robert his prisoner, and kept him confined during the remainder of his life, which was twenty-eight years.

Robert had a son, William, of whom Henry was very jealous, fearing he would one day get possession of the throne, to the exclusion of his own son. He made every effort to get possession of his person, but without success. His whole life was harassed with anxiety to secure the crown to his darling son. And, to prevent any other from claiming it, he caused all his Barons to swear fealty to him, during his own life. But all his care and anxiety were vain and fruitless. His son, died in the eighteenth year of his age. He was crossing over from Normandy to England, in a ship, called "the White Ship." The captain, whose name was Fitzstephen, suffered his men to drink so freely of the young Prince's wine, that they all became intoxicated, and incapable of doing their duty. The ship was consequently run ashore, and all on board, except one man, perished. When the captain saw the danger they were in, he put the Prince into a boat, with a few young nobles; and they might have reached the shore in safety—but the Prince, hearing the shrieks of his sister, the countess of Perche, insisted on going back for her. So many persons jumped in, that the boat sunk, and all were lost.

Henry now became as anxious to secure the crown for his daughter Matilda, as he had been for his son William. But in this also he was doomed to be disappointed, as the next reign will show.

STEPHEN.

FOURTH NORMAN.

1136.

STEPHEN.

STEPHEN was the favourite nephew of Henry, and had received from him large estates, and many other kindnesses. But, notwithstanding this, as soon as he heard of his uncle's death, he hastened to England, and usurped the crown. This was so unexpected and sudden, that Matilda, (or the Empress Maude, as she is generally called, because she was the wife of Henry V. Emperor of Germany,) was taken wholly by surprise. As soon as she could collect herself, she made great efforts to regain her rights. Her brother, the Earl of Gloucester, assisted her. Some of the Barons sided with her, and some with Stephen; and, for several years, England was desolated with one of the most calamitous wars it ever knew. At one time, in 1141, Stephen was taken prisoner, and Maude acknowledged Queen; but, she made herself so disagreeable to the people, that, before the preparations for her coronation were completed, she was obliged to fly. Her brother, endeavouring to follow her, was taken prisoner, but was soon exchanged for Stephen. Maude was now so closely pursued, that, at one time, she escaped only by being borne on a litter, like a corpse. At another time, her garrison being reduced by famine, and the ground covered with snow, Maude, and three of her knights, dressing themselves wholly in white, so as not to be seen, got out of the castle in the night, crossed the river on the ice, and so made their escape. In 1147, the Earl of Gloucester died. Wearied and discouraged, Maude now resigned her claims to her son Henry; and an arrangement was soon made with Stephen, that he should retain the throne during his life, and then leave it to Henry.

HENRY II.

FIRST PLANTAGENET.

1154.

HENRY II.

Henry II., son of Maude, was descended from the Saxon kings, and from this time the Saxons have held possession of the throne. He was surnamed Plantagenet, because he wore in his helmet a sprig of the *planta genista*, or broom. He was not only king of England, but had a large domain in France.

Ireland was at this time divided into five petty kingdoms. Dermot, one of the kings, being driven from his throne, came over to England in 1171, to ask assistance of Henry, to recover it. The Earl of Pembroke, surnamed Strongbow, with a few other noblemen, went over, and soon restored Dermot to his kingdom. Dermot then asked them to assist him in conquering the other four kingdoms. They consented, Strongbow at the same time marrying Eva, the daughter of Dermot. When they had conquered the king of Meath, Dermot died, and Strongbow, as his son, became king. He, however, resigned his power to Henry, who went over himself the next year, with a great force, and subdued the whole island.

Thomas à Becket was a very distinguished person in this reign. He was the so[n of a ?] common citizen of London, but became so [great a] favorite of the king, that he made him Chancellor, and afterwards Archbishop of Canterbury. He is said to have been very extravagant in his expenses, and to have indulged in every kind of luxury and magnificence. To show what was meant by luxury and extravagance in those days, it is mentioned, as an instance of Becket's extreme delicacy, that in winter, his rooms were every day covered with clean hay and straw, and in summer with green rushes, or boughs, so that his visitors should not soil their fine clothes by sitting on a dirty floor.

Becket at length became so arrogant, that the king was quite out of patience with him, and some of his knights, thinking it would gratify their master to be rid of him, pursued him into the cathedral, and slew him on the steps of the altar.

Henry's sons entered into a conspiracy with the kings of France and Scotland, to dethrone him, and queen Eleanor, Henry's wife, encouraged them in it. The king having defeated them all, pardoned his sons, but shut up his wife in close confinement. Notwithstanding his father's kindness, Henry, the oldest son, and heir to the throne, rebelled again, and raised an army against his father; but becoming sick and finding himself about to die, he was so deeply affected with grief and shame for his ungrateful conduct, that he caused himself to be laid on a heap of ashes, with a halter about his neck, and so died.

HENRY II. 35

Richard now became heir to the throne, and he soon raised a rebellion against his father, joined by his brother John, and Philip, king of France. This troubled Henry so much, that it threw him into a fever, of which he died.

Henry's family sorrows were many, and not undeserved, since he had chosen to take for his queen a woman of very bad character, merely for ambition's sake; and then when he found himself unhappy, he sought the company of other women.

Among others, there was one very beautiful girl called Rosamond, whom King Henry loved extremely, and because he dreaded lest the queen should ill treat her if she found out his attachment, he concealed her in a labyrinth in Woodstock Park.

The queen after some time discovered the secret of this labyrinth, and found her way quite into fair Rosamond's presence; and, when there, held out a bowl of poison to Rosamond, and obliged her to drink it, while she held a dagger to her breast. But if she hoped, when her rival was gone, that King Henry would love her better, she was very much mistaken, since he could not but hate her cruelty, and mourn for poor Rosamond. Besides this, the queen made him miserable by her bad temper, and by constantly leading his sons to quarrel with him and with one another.

Paper, of recent invention, began to be used in this reign, and was of great advantage in the progress of learning.

4

RICHARD I.

SECOND PLANTAGENET.

1189.

RICHARD CŒUR DE LION.

Richard, was surnamed Cœur de Lion, or lion hearted, from his great courage and his generous disposition. One of his first acts was to release his mother from her long confinement. He bestowed many favors on his brother John, for which he afterwards showed himself very ungrateful. But the great business of Richard's life was the crusade. Jerusalem after having been in possession of the Christians about one hundred years, had just been recovered by the Mahometans, under Saladin, Sultan of Egypt. The news of this disaster threw all Europe into consternation, and the nations aroused themselves, with the greatest ardor, to recover the holy place. Richard took with him all the men and money he could raise. On his way he conquered Cyprus, which he afterwards gave to Guy of Lusignan, as a compensation for the loss of the empty title of King of Jerusalem, which was given to Conrad of Montserrat. He then joined the other christian forces at Acre, which was in possession of the Christians, and besieged by Saladin. Gaining a complete victory here, they then attacked and took Joppa, and would have gone at once to Jerusalem; but, owing to unhappy differences between Richard and Philip of France, who had previously deserted the cause, instructing the Duke of Burgundy whom he left behind, to omit no opportunity to thwart and mortify Richard, the army was broken up, and the whole project defeated. Richard, left alone, and falling sick, concluded a truce with Saladin. On his way home, attempting to pass through Germany in the disguise of a pilgrim, he was so lavish of his money, that they suspected his disguise, and made him prisoner. He was treated very unkindly, and afterwards ransomed for 150,000 marks. On his return to England, he was received with great joy. But he immediately engaged in a war with Philip of France, which continued, with some intervals, for four years, and was at last terminated, by the mediation of the Pope.

He died in the year 1199 of a wound received while beseiging a castle in Normandy, called Chaluz.

The wound was given by a soldier, who was taken prisoner and brought before the king, and the king asked him "why he had sought to take his life?"

"Because," said the soldier, "you killed my father and brother. I have but taken a just revenge."

Richard, far from being incensed by this reply, pardoned the soldier, and ordered a present to be given him; but after he was dead his generals disobeyed his orders, and put the poor soldier to a miserable death.

4

JOHN.

THIRD PLANTAGENET.

1199.

JOHN LACKLAND.

John was mean, perfidious and cruel, and had so little capacity, that he was scarcely more able to manage his private affairs, than those of the nation. He ordered his nephew, Arthur of Bretagne, to be put to death, but finding his order was not executed, murdered him with his own hands. This made him an object of universal detestation; and, partly because his barons refused to assist him against Philip of France, and partly from his own cowardice and sloth, he lost Normandy and nearly all his other possessions in France, which procured him the surname of Lackland. John had a quarrel with the Pope, who first laid the kingdom under an *interdict*, and then *excommunicated* the king. When a nation was under an *interdict*, the churches were shut, the bells could not be rung, nor the dead buried, except in ditches and holes, without service. When a person was *excommunicated*, whether king or subject, all persons were forbidden to do him any kind of service, or to come near him. This sentence was soon recalled, and John laid his crown at the feet of the Pope's legate, who kicked it from him. His Barons now conspired against him, and compelled him to sign a bill of rights and privileges, which greatly limited the power of the king. This bill is called the *Magna Charta*, and is the fountain head of all English liberty. It was drawn up by Stephen Langton, Archbishop of Canterbury, and signed at Runimede, on the 15th of June, 1215.

The famous Robin Hood lived at this time, and gave the king and the nobles great trouble, by killing game, which they claimed the sole right to kill. He and his band were called "outlaws." They were favourites of the people, for they robbed only the rich, and were kind to the poor.

If a rich, purse-proud abbot, or some very wealthy merchant, was known to be passing through the forests, Robin Hood was sure to have notice of it, and to be ready to waylay him, and demand a certain portion of his money.

On the contrary, if a poor distressed pilgrim went his way through Sherwood Forest, and fell in with Robin, he was certain of courteous treatment, of a hearty meal, and perhaps a handsome present to boot.

Robin Hood's archers were so skilful in the use of the bow, as to perform feats which seem to us incredible. It is even said, that both Robin and his friend Little John could shoot an arrow a measured mile.

They were all dressed in cloth of Lincoln Green, and had their own laws and regulations. Robin was never captured or conquered, but was treacherously bled to death, by a woman to whom he committed himself in a fit of illness.

HENRY III.

FOURTH PLANTAGENET.

1216.

HENRY OF WINCHESTER.

HENRY III. born at Winchester, was only eight years old, when his father died. The Earl of Pembroke was Protector two years, and after his death, Hubert de Burgh and Peter de Roches. At the age of 16 Henry was declared of age. About this time, the Pope interfered very much in the affairs of England. He drew Henry into a war with Sicily. The Barons, under Simon de Montfort, raised a rebellion. The king made many conditions, but broke them as soon as they were made. The country was distracted with wars for several years. Henry and his son, Prince Edward, were made prisoners by De Montfort, who tried to raise himself to the throne.

The Earl of Gloucester favored the king, and contrived a plan to set Prince Edward at liberty. Edward pretended to be sick, and obtained leave to ride out, for the benefit of his health. He was furnished with a very fleet horse by Gloucester; and, after riding several hard races with his guards, till their horses were tired out, he politely bade them good bye, and putting spurs to his horse, was soon out of sight. The two parties met soon after at Evesham, May 4, 1265, where the Prince was victorious, the king rescued, and the power of the Barons broken.—After this, Prince Edward went on a crusade to the Holy Land. The Saracens found him so powerful an enemy, that they employed a man to assassinate him. He would have been killed by the poisoned weapon, but his wife Eleanora sucked the poison from the wound, and saved his life.

Henry III. signed the Magna Charta as soon as he was old enough to understand it; but he never entered into the spirit of it.

He repeatedly broke his promises to the barons, and they determined to make him renew them in a more solemn manner. They therefore assembled in great pomp in Westminster Hall, and the Charter was read.

At the end of it there was a solemn sentence of excommunication against any who should break it; and when this sentence was pronounced, all the prelates, who had burning tapers in their hands, cast them down, exclaiming, "So may all that incur this sentence be extinguished in hell;" and the king added, "So help me God, I will keep these things as I am a man: as I am a Christian: as I am a knight: as I am a king, crowned and anointed."

The first parliament was held in this reign, called together by De Montfort, in the king's name. The Newcastle mines were opened. Gunpowder was discovered by Roger Bacon, but not applied to any use. Bacon was so learned that he was looked upon as a magician, and imprisoned as such for many years.

EDWARD I.

FIFTH PLANTAGENET.

1272.

EDWARD I.

EDWARD was in Palestine, when his father died. Immediately on his return he set about contriving means to raise money, by robbing his people. If he found any man who had not a *written title* to his estate, he made him pay a large fine, or forfeit his estate. The Earl of Warrenne, when called upon to produce his title, drew an old rusty sword, and said "by this my fathers gained their estates, and by this I will keep it." This alarmed Edward, and he went no farther.

Llewellyn, king of Wales, being a troublesome neighbor, Edward made war upon him, defeated and killed him; and promising to the people a prince of their own country, who could not speak English, presented to them his eldest son, born a few days before at Carnarvon. From that time the king's eldest son has been called the Prince of Wales.

There was great trouble in Scotland at this time. There were thirteen competitors for the crown. Robert Bruce and John Baliol were the most powerful, and they referred to Edward to decide between them. He first required all Scotland to submit to him, and then decided in favor of Baliol, who became a mere tool in his hands. The Scots resisted, and William Wallace kept up the struggle for eight years. Wallace gathered his countrymen together; he drove out Edward's governors; he got possession of the principal towns: and it was seven years before the King of England succeeded in conquering this brave man.

But Wallace himself was at length betrayed into the hands of Edward by a false friend, and the king, who only saw in him an enemy, and felt no respect for his devoted exertions for his country, treated him like a common malefactor, sent him up to London, where he was hung, and his head afterwards exposed on London Bridge. After this, Bruce, the younger, kept up the contest for two years, or more, when Edward vowed he would not leave Scotland, till he had subdued it. He met with great opposition from the hardy Scots, and finally, when but little progress had been made, fell ill and died on the road side, near Carlisle, July 7, 1307.

What you have heard of Edward the First has not been much to his credit; and yet he had some very good points in his character: an excellent son, a good master, and a faithful friend; not given to ostentation, but very simple in his dress and appearance. He attached his relations and friends strongly to him, though so stern to his enemies.

As a father, however, he was not happy. He spoiled his eldest boy, allowing him in too much indulgence and luxury: and this weak and unfortunate man, who was called Edward the Second, and sometimes Edward of Caernarvon, led a very unhappy life, and came to a miserable death in the year 1328.

EDWARD II.

SIXTH PLANTAGENET.

1307.

EDWARD OF CAERNARVON.

EDWARD II. born at Caernarvon in Wales, was a weak, passionate and intemperate prince. Under his reign England, was again distracted with civil wars. The Barons hated him, and raised a rebellion, and compelled him to submit to their terms. In the mean time, the intrepid Bruce had established himself on the throne of Scotland, and had driven the English from nearly all their strong holds there. Edward roused himself, and thought to conquer Scotland at a blow. He raised an immense army. Bruce met them at Bannockburn, with only 30,000 men, and put them completely to rout.

About ten years after this, another rebellion broke out, headed by the queen, Isabella, the daughter of Philip of France. Many of the nobles joined, and the Prince of Wales, then 14 years old, was placed at the head of the army, and declared regent. They soon got possession of the king, who had vainly sought refuge, first in Wales, then in Ireland, and then in some of the monasteries of England. He was deposed, and his son proclaimed king. But the prince refused to be king, without his father's consent. This was forced from him, and the miserable man was put under the care of keepers, who treated him with the greatest indignity and unkindness.

Thus ended the reign of Edward the Second, a period of public disgrace and private calamity. But his own miseries did not end with his abdication of the crown. After his deposition, he was first put under the care of the Earl of Lancaster; but the queen thinking he was treated too humanely, transferred him to three other keepers, who were to keep him each a month by turns. One of these used him kindly; but the other two, hoping thereby to gain favor with the queen, seemed desirous to kill him by ill usage. They hurried him from castle to castle, in the middle of the night, and but half clothed. One day they ordered him to be shaved with water out of a dirty ditch, and would not allow him any other.

The varied insults and cruelties did not satisfy the cruel and unrelenting queen. She therefore gave orders to have him put to death, without delay. This order was executed, with circumstances of great cruelty, on the 21st. of September, 1327, in the forty-third year of the king's age.

EDWARD III.

SEVENTH PLANTAGENET.

1327.

EDWARD III.

EDWARD III. was a man of great capacities, and very ambitious. His queen, Philippa, of Hainault, was also remarkable for her talents and virtues. Edward made war against Scotland, and took David, son of Robert Bruce, a prisoner, and placed the son of Baliol on the throne. He then laid claim to France, as nephew to the late king, and a long and desperate war ensued. The first important battle was that of Cressy, in which the Prince of Wales, called the Black Prince, because he wore black armor, with 30,000 men, defeated Philip with 100,000. This victory was partly owing to gunpowder, which was now used for the first time in war. Then followed the famous siege of Calais. This lasted nearly a year, till the people were so reduced that they had to eat horses, dogs, and cats, and when this failed, they surrendered. Edward required that six of the principal citizens should come out to him barefooted, with ropes round their necks, and bring him the keys of the town, and he would spare the lives of all the rest. Eustace de Pierre, one of the richest merchants of the place, and five others, offered themselves as victims. Edward ordered them at once to be executed. But queen Philippa fell on her knees before him, and begged him to pardon them. The king granted her request, when she took them to her apartments, entertained them honorably, and sent them back to their friends. Edward took possession of Calais, drove out all the old inhabitants, and filled it with his own people.—For the next six years, a terrible pestilence, called the Black death, raged throughout Europe. After this, the war with France was renewed by the Black Prince. In 1356, the battle of Poitiers was fought between the Black Prince, with 12,000 and King John, with 60,000, in which the French were entirely defeated, and king John and his son taken prisoners. They were carried to England, and treated with the greatest respect and sympathy, more like distinguished visiters, than prisoners. Edward had now two captive kings in his possession; but, in the course of the same year, David Bruce was set at liberty, and the king of France ransomed for 3,000,000 of gold crowns. Forty noblemen were sent to England to be held as hostages, till the money was paid. One of these, making his escape, John, who felt his own honor impeached by this breach of faith, returned to England to give himself up to Edward, and falling ill of a fever, died there in 1364.

The Black Prince died in 1375. His death was lamented by all the English, as a public calamity. It broke the heart of the old king, his father, who died about a year afterwards.

RICHARD II.

EIGHTH PLANTAGENET.

1377.

RICHARD OF BORDEAUX.

RICHARD II., son of the Black Prince, born at Bordeaux, was in his twelfth year, when he came to the throne. His uncle, John of Gaunt, was his chief counsellor. The people, feeling themselves too heavily taxed to support the king's expenses, raised an insurrection, under Wat Tyler and Jack Straw. With these leaders, a mob of three hundred thousand men, marched into London, and committed great violence. The King, young as he was, went out to meet them, unarmed, and behaved with so much courage and prudence, that the mob was soon dispersed. But this was almost the only instance, during his whole life, in which he conducted like a king. He was a weak, foolish man, for many years the mere tool of his uncle the duke of Gloucester.

Richard's reign soon became troubled, and graver difficulties crowded upon him. The Commons, who, by the law of the realm, were justified in remonstrating against his ministers, now set themselves steadily to oppose their illegal acts.

The king is said to have remarked upon this, that he would not remove the lowest scullion in his kitchen to please them; but the Lords and Commons both uniting together, he was obliged to give way and dismiss his chancellor.

Eight years passed away in continual quarrels; and though the king sought to amuse the court and people with a magnificent tournament, and with many other splendid sights, he could not regain the confidence of his parliament.

But the worst of his actions was the murder of his uncle, the Duke of Gloucester, whom he cruelly himself betrayed into an ambush which he had planned for him, and caused him to be conveyed to Calais and killed.

His excuse for this wicked act, was, that the Duke meant to murder him. From this time he was justly regarded as a tyrant, and took the precautions of one; for he was always guarded by two hundred bowmen wherever he went.

It was not long after this act that he banished two noblemen, one the Duke of Norfolk, and the other Henry of Lancaster, his uncle's son, who, with the aid of the Duke of York, raised a rebellion, made the king prisoner, and then compelled him to abdicate in 1399. He is supposed to have been murdered soon after.

Wickliffe flourished at this time, and translated the Bible into English. They had none but Latin Bibles before, and those only in the hands of the priests.

Geoffery Chaucer, who is called the father of English poetry, lived during this reign.

HENRY IV.

NINTH PLANTAGENET.

1399.

HENRY BOLINGBROKE.

Henry IV. was the only son of John of Gaunt. He had no right to the throne. The true heir was Edmund Mortimer, Earl of March, at that time seven years old. Henry, having been banished by Richard, took advantage of the general disaffection among the people, raised a rebellion, and placed himself on the throne. He was the first king of the house of Lancaster.

A rebellion was raised in Wales, under Owen Glendower, which kept Henry in trouble for seven years. The Scots, under Earl Douglas, also invaded England, but were defeated by the Percies, the Earl of Northumberland, and his son Henry Hotspur. No sooner was this done, than the Percies, offended at the king's treatment, in relation to the ransom of prisoners, set Douglas at liberty, and called in Owen Glendower to join them in dethroning Henry. On the 21st of July, 1403, the great battle of Shrewsbury was fought, in which Hotspur was killed, and the rebel army defeated.—Two years after, there was another rebellion, headed by Scroop, Archbishop of York, and Thomas Mowbray. Ralph Nevil, Earl of Westmoreland, was sent against them. Finding them too numerous to hazard a battle, he sent a message, promising to redress all their grievances. Satisfied with this, they began to disperse. As soon as the camp was broken, he seized the leaders, and caused them all to be beheaded.—In 1415, the son of the king of Scotland (afterwards James I.,) fell into the hands of Henry. He was a prisoner eighteen years, and was then ransomed, and placed on the throne of his fathers. While in England, he received a good education. He had a great talent for music and poetry, and is supposed to be the author of that sweet and plaintive style of music, which is peculiar to Scotland.

Several of the Lollards were burnt as heretics, in this reign. The Lollards were followers of Wickliffe, and were put to death because they did not believe that the Pope could pardon sin, and that the bread and wine used at the sacrament, were the *real body* and *blood* of Christ.

Henry the Fourth was much impressed with the desire to go on a crusade to the Holy Land. But he fell into bad health, was subject to epileptic fits, and sometimes was so bereft of sense or motion, that he was believed to be dead. On one of these occasions, his son Henry came into the room, and seeing the crown on a cushion near the bed, carried it away. The king shortly after revived, and, calling his son, said, with a sigh, " My son, what right had you to it? you know that *I* had none." "My Lord," answered Henry, " you won it by your sword, and so will I hold and defend it during my life." The king answered, " Well, as you see best. I leave all things to God, and pray that He would have mercy upon me." And shortly after, without uttering another word, he expired, in the fourteenth year of his reign.

HENRY V.

TENTH PLANTAGENET.

1413.

HENRY V.

HENRY V. had been a wild and dissipated youth. On coming to the throne, he abandoned all his youthful follies, and forbade his former companions to come near him, till they too reformed. He generously set at liberty, Edmund Mortimer, the real heir to the throne, and recalled the son of Hotspur from exile, and restored to him the estates and honors of his family. But he showed great cruelty, in causing Lord Cobham to be burnt as a heretic.

In 1415, Henry invaded France. After capturing and garrisoning Harfleur, he set out to return to England, but was met, near Azincourt, by the duke of Orleans, with one hundred thousand men. Henry's force was only ten thousand. He sent David Gam, a Welshman, to report the number of the enemy. His report was that "there were enough to fight, enough to be killed, and enough to run away." The battle was a most desperate and bloody one, and, though the French were ten to one of the English, they met with an utter defeat. The duke d'Alençon, and eighteen other French knights had made an oath to kill or take Henry. But they all lost their lives in the attempt, being killed by David Gam, and two other Welshmen, who defended the king, at the expense of their own lives. Henry knighted them all, as they lay bleeding to death at his feet.—In 1417, Henry made another attack upon France, conquered the whole of Normandy, and, taking advantage of the factions among the nobles, procured himself to be acknowledged as Regent of France, with the right of succession, on the death of the reigning king.

There was much to admire in the character of Henry the Fifth, when we consider the time in which he lived. He was kind to the poor, and firmly maintained justice; hence the poor every where loved him. He would not suffer his noblemen and gentlemen to trample on them; and even while in France, in a hostile country, he was so careful of the lower classes that they suffered much less by his followers than by their own nobles.

Thus, though a foreigner and usurper, he was really popular in France. But he did not escape the bigoted notions and practices of his time, and considered that no better atonement could be made for sin, than the persecution of heretics. He even personally attended at the burning of one for heresy. He took infinite pains to convert him, but when he found it was all in vain, and that the poor man persisted in his belief, he left him to his fate. Henry died in 1422. Tapers were kept burning, day and night, on his tomb, for nearly a century.

HENRY VI.

ELEVENTH PLANTAGENET.

1422.

HENRY VI.

Henry VI. was not a year old, at the death of his father. He was placed under the care of the Earl of Warwick. The duke of Bedford was regent of France, and the duke of Gloucester regent of England. The king of France, who had been insane, died soon after, and his son, as Charles VII. put forward his claims to the throne. The English had possession of Paris, and proceeded to lay siege to Orleans. They had nearly reduced the place by famine, when it was relieved, and the whole aspect of the war changed in a most remarkable manner. A poor peasant girl, eighteen years of age, named Joan of Arc, or "the Maid of Orleans," conceiving that she was designed by heaven to save her country, procured admission to Charles, and succeeded in persuading him and his counsellors to endue her with the proper authority to relieve Orleans. She had a splendid banner prepared, with the figure of the Saviour upon it, and proclaimed herself, as commissioned from heaven to save France. She then forced her way into Orleans, encouraged the poor citizens, and finally led them out to assault the beseigers. The English were as much disheartened, as the French were animated, by the idea of her supernatural powers; so that she soon drove them away from all their fortifications, and procured Charles to be crowned at Rheims. The English, at the same time, had Henry crowned at Paris, being only six years old. The French almost worshipped their deliverer, and the king ennobled her and her family by the name of "Des Lys." But, shortly after, on a slight reverse of fortune at Compeigne, she was cruelly left to fall into the hands of her enemies, the English, who, more cruelly still, burnt her alive, as a Witch.

Henry VI. was of a mild and amiable disposition, and would much rather have been a shepherd than a king. He married Margaret of Anjou, a woman of an ambitious and vindictive temper. Henry was of the House of Lancaster, that usurped the throne, the second reign previous to this. The duke of York, in whose family the line should have descended, now set up his claims, and thus commenced those long and desolating civil wars, known as the "Wars of the Roses," because York assumed as a badge the White Rose, and Lancaster the Red. The country was in a sad state of commotion. Mobs and tumults were on every side, the most formidable of these was headed by the famous Jack Cade, and at one time threatened London with pillage.

The Duke of York was killed, in one of the many battles that wasted the country—but his son Edward pursued his claim, till he defeated the Lancastrians in 1461, and was proclaimed king.

EDWARD IV.

TWELFTH PLANTAGENET.

1461.

EDWARD IV.

EDWARD IV. was 19 years old when he came to the throne. He was cruel and vindictive, condemning as a traitor every Lancastrian, who fell into his hands. The "Wars of the Roses" continued to ravage the country. The old king, Henry VI. was in prison, but Margaret, his queen, made every exertion in favour of her son. The Earl of Warwick, the last and the most powerful of the Barons, had, till now, favoured the house of York. But being offended because Edward made what he considered an improper marriage, he joined the Duke of Clarence, Edward's brother, in a conspiracy against him. He also connected Margaret with them, by marrying his daughter Anne with Prince Edward her son. This came so suddenly upon Edward, that he was obliged to fly, and Warwick carried all before him. Poor Henry VI. was dragged from prison, and once more made king, in 1471. In a few months, however, Edward was restored, and Henry committed to the Tower, where he was soon after secretly murdered by the Duke of Gloucester. The two parties fought several battles, after this, in one of which Clarence deserted and went over to his brother, and the great Warwick was killed. In another, Margaret and Prince Edward were taken prisoners, and thus ended the wars of the roses, in which, in the course of eighteen years, sixty royal princes, more than half the nobles of the country, and one hundred thousand of the people, were killed.

The Duke of Clarence having spoken disrespectfully of the king, was condemned to death. As a special favor, he was allowed to choose the manner of his death, and was accordingly, at his request, drowned in a butt of malmsey.

It was during this reign, in the year 1474, that William Caxton, the first English printer, set up the first printing-press in London, somewhere near to Westminster Abbey.

Printing had been invented and practised on the Continent about thirty-six years before, and books printed abroad had been brought to England, but no Englishman had attempted to set up the business before Caxton.

We, who live at a time when books are cheap and plentiful, can scarcely form an idea of the cost of forming even a very small collection of useful volumes, when all had to be copied by hand.

Books were so valuable that it was very difficult to borrow or procure what was wanted, and people were obliged to deposit money in pledge, when they took one out of a library.

EDWARD V.

THIRTEENTH PLANTAGENET.

1483.

EDWARD V.

EDWARD V. was 13 years old when his father died. His uncle, Richard, Duke of Gloucester, the same who murdered poor Henry VI. in the Tower, had long had an eye upon the throne, and found this a good opportunity to seize it. He was deformed in person, but more so in heart, selfish, deceitful and cruel. He immediately seized the young king, and pretending to be his friend, had him proclaimed king, and himself appointed Protector. In this he was assisted by Lord Hastings; but no sooner was he made protector, than he had Hastings beheaded as a traitor, together with Lords Rivers and Grey, Edward's guardians. He then got possession of Edward's only brother, the young Duke of York, under pretence of having him present at his brother's coronation. Having them both in his power, Gloucester now declared to the people, that the late king, his brother, had been married to another lady, previously to his marriage with the mother of these boys, and consequently they were neither of them legitimately entitled to the throne. By this, and other artifices, the people of London were induced to offer the crown to Richard. At first he affected to refuse it, after the example of Cæsar, saying that he loved his brother's children more than he loved a crown. His pretended reluctance, however, soon gave way to the urgent persuasions of the Duke of Buckingham. He was at once proclaimed king, and the preparations which had been making for the coronation of the youthful Edward, served for that of his cruel and hypocritical uncle.

The two unfortunate young princes were no sooner in Richard's power, than they were sent to that prison and tomb of England's princes and noblemen—the Tower. Their fate was for a long time involved in obscurity. They were never more seen, and probably would never have been heard of again, had it not been necessary, some ten years after, in order to defeat the claims of an imposter, to make public the proof of their death. It was then shown by the testimony of two persons, who acknowledged that they were accessory to the murder, that they had been suffocated in their bed, and buried at the foot of a stair case in the Tower.

They survived their father about three months.

RICHARD III.

FOURTEENTH PLANTAGENET.

1483.

RICHARD III.

THIS execrable king had but little enjoyment during the two brief years of his reign. A conspiracy was soon formed to place Henry Tudor, the Earl of Richmond, on the throne. Richard's only child died about the same time, for which his grief was so excessive, that he almost lost his reason. The Tudors were of Welsh origin, and Richmond made many friends in Wales. At one time, he was near being discovered by one of Richard's spies, and only saved himself by jumping out of a back window, and getting through a hole, which is still called "the king's hole."* At length, collecting their forces, the two parties met at Bosworth, August 22, 1485. Richard was hated by the people, and many deserted to Richmond during the night. When the battle commenced in the morning, Lord Stanley, Richard's chief commander, turned his arms upon the king. Seeing that all was lost, and exclaiming "treason! treason!" Richard made a desperate plunge into the midst of the enemy, hoping to kill Richmond. The Earl

* The following riddle alludes to this event:—
"Some rise by climbing, some by creeping,
And many a *hole* has crowns in keeping;
And he who, when he must, will crawl,
May gain a throne, or save a fall."

shrunk back from the madman, but his attendants closed in upon Richard, who fought like a wild beast at bay, and fell covered with wounds. Thus ended the dynasty of the Plantagenets, who had held the throne during fourteen successive reigns.

A work just issued from the press in England, which we have not seen, undertakes the defence of Richard's character, endeavoring, as one of the Reviews remarks, to make it out that he has been slandered by the historians, while he was, in fact, no worse than kings in general.

He was a warlike, ambitious man, and had been brought up, like all the men of that time, in war and bloodshed. Hence he probably committed as many bad acts as they did.

But *he* has been dealt with more hardly than others, because all the writers who have given us his history for several reigns afterwards, lived under princes of the Lancastrian line, which had supplanted his.

They, therefore, were hardly fair persons, being of that party which was opposed to the Yorkists; and it was natural both that some of these should be inclined to pay court to the reigning party, while others merely took things as they heard from common report.

Making all these allowances, however, I believe Richard the Third to have made no conscience of committing any act by which he could secure the crown.

HENRY VII.

FIRST TUDOR.

1485.

HENRY OF RICHMOND.

RICHARD had gone into battle with the crown on his head. As soon as he fell, Lord Stanley took the crown, battered and broken as it was, and placed it on the head of Richmond, and the field resounded with shouts of "Long live king Henry!"

One of the Plantagenets remained, whom Henry hated and feared. This was Edward, Earl of Warwick, son of that Duke of Clarence who was drowned in a butt of malmsey. The first command he gave, as king, even on the bloody field, was to have this poor boy conveyed to the Tower. His cruelty soon raised him enemies.

A boy named Lambert Simnel, son of a baker at Oxford, was taught to personate the young Earl of Warwick, and was actually proclaimed king, in Dublin, as Edward VI. This plot was soon defeated, and the pretended king became a scullion in Henry's kitchen.

After this another impostor arose, named Perkin Warbeck. He strongly resembled the Plantagenets, and undertook to personate the young Duke of York, brother of Edward V. who, they now pretended, was not suffocated with his brother, but had escaped from the Tower. He gained many friends, and among others, James IV. of Scotland, who gave him in marriage, Lady Catharine Douglass, one of the most noble families in Scotland. James entered England with an army, but Henry contrived to detach him from Warbeck, and draw him into a treaty with himself.—Warbeck was soon after taken and conveyed to the Tower. Here he contrived to hold some communication with the poor Earl of Warwick, and to concert a plan for their escape. The plan was discovered, and they were both executed.

Columbus discovered America, about this time, and when Henry heard of it, he sent a fleet of ships, under John Cabot, a Venetian merchant, to make further discoveries. They discovered Newfoundland and St. John's, and sailed as far as Virginia.

The reign of Henry VII. is generally considered the dawn of English liberty. The Magna Charta had done much to protect the nobles from the tyrranny of the king, but little had as yet been done to protect the common people against the oppression of the nobles: the long civil wars had now, however, greatly curtailed their power, and Henry made it a part of his policy still further to depress them. This he did by restricting the number of their retainers; thus compelling large numbers of men, whose whole business had been fighting, to apply themselves to some industrial art for a living. And soon, from being helpless dependants upon some great Baron, or turbulent disturbers of the peace, they became useful subjects and quiet neighbours.

HENRY VIII.

SECOND TUDOR.

1509.

HENRY VIII.

HENRY VIII. came to the throne at 19 years of age. His father was a Lancaster, and his mother a York, so that his title to the throne was undisputed.

Wolsey, the son of a butcher, but a very shrewd man, became a great favorite, and acquired unbounded influence. He was soon made Archbishop, Chancellor, Cardinal, and then aimed to be made Pope.

In 1524, Henry wrote a book against Luther, for which the Pope gave him the title of "Defender of the Faith."

Henry was six times married. His first wife was Catharine of Arragon. Her he divorced in 1533, and married Anne Boleyn. The Pope opposed Henry in this, and Henry, by way of retaliation, called a parliament, and had laws passed, denying the supremacy of the Pope. This divorced the Church of England from the Church of Rome, and the union has never been renewed, except during the few years of Mary's reign.

About this time, Wolsey lost all his favor and is honors. Thomas Cranmer rose to be Archbishop of Canterbury. Sir Thomas More was made Chancellor, in place of Wolsey. Anne Boleyn, without any sufficient cause, was beheaded in

1536, and the king was the next day married to Jane Seymour. She died in less than a year. Anne of Cleves was Henry's next wife. Seeing a portrait of her, which represented her as very beautiful, he sent to demand her in marriage. But not finding her as beautiful as the picture, he immediately divorced her, and, a fortnight after, married Catharine Howard. She did not retain his favor long, but was beheaded in 1542. Even after this, another woman was found, courageous enough to be this Blue-Beard's sixth wife; and this was Catharine Parr. She, however, managed the king better than his other wives had done, and as Henry was grown infirm and diseased, she became necessary to him as a nurse and attendant. But even with all her patience and good management, she was once in great danger of losing her life: the king had gone so far as to sign an order for her being sent to prison, but she diverted his mind from the idea.

The separation of the English Church from that of Rome was followed by the breaking up of the monasteries, and the dispersion of the monks and nuns. This led to great disturbances. Henry was very tyrannical and capricious, many of the best and most accomplished men in the kingdom were put to death for their religious opinions. Among these Sir Thomas More and Lord Surrey were distinguished. By the influence of Cranmer, English prayers were first introduced into the service of the Church.—The English first engaged in the slave trade in this reign.

EDWARD VI.

THIRD TUDOR.

1547.

EDWARD VI.

EDWARD VI. was ten years old when his father died. He was the son of Jane Seymour. His father had appointed sixteen executors, and eighteen counsellors, to whom he entrusted the care of the king, and the kingdom. But, at their first meeting they deviated from the king's instructions, by making the Duke of Somerset Protector. The duke was a Protestant, and took care to place the young king's education in the hands of good men. Cranmer was one of them. . Edward was a very clever, intelligent youth, of a serious mind and sound judgment, and Cranmer found no difficulty in interesting him in the religious changes which were then in progress. Almost the whole attention of the government was directed to the Reformation of the Church. A book of Common Prayer was prepared, the 39 articles adopted,* and the liturgy was arranged nearly as it is now.

In 1549, Somerset resigned the Protectorship, and the Earl of Warwick was appointed in his stead. Warwick had more zeal than Somerset. He was

* The articles, as originally prepared by Cranmer, were forty-two, but were afterwards reduced to thirty-nine.

also very selfish and ambitious. He persuaded Edward to make him Duke of Northumberland, and to give him all the vast estates of that ancient Earldom. By his influence Gardiner and Bonner were imprisoned as Catholics, and the princess Mary, threatened with punishment, for persisting in her conformity to the Romish Church, She was however, permitted, to have mass performed privately in her house.

Edward was very desirous to cut off Mary from the succession, on account of her religious opinions, and the bigotry which she manifested in regard to them. He therefore, by the advice of Warwick, settled the succession on Lady Jane Grey, whom Warwick had procured to be married to his son, Guilford Dudley.

Edward died soon after, at 16 years of age.— Pins were invented in this, or the preceding reign, and were found a great convenience to the ladies.

It would puzzle many, at the present day, to know how ladies could get along without so necessary an article. A variety of contrives were resorted to, some of which, such as buttons, and hooks and eyes, are still in use. But *wooden skewers* have probably quite gone out of fashion. Needles were rare in the reign of Henry 6th: none were made in England till the succeeding reign, when a Spanish negro commenced the manufacture of them in London.

MARY.

FOURTH TUDOR.

1553.

MARY.

As soon as Edward was dead, the Duke of Northumberland had Lady Jane Grey proclaimed as Queen. She had previously married his son, Lord Dudley. The people, however, acknowledged Mary, the daughter of Catharine. Northumberland was beheaded at once. Lady Jane, and Lord Dudley, after a reign of ten days, were imprisoned about a year, and then beheaded. Lady Jane's father was beheaded soon after. The Church was now reunited to Rome; Gardiner and Bonner were liberated, and Cardinal de la Pole appointed legate to England. Mary married Philip of Spain, son of Charles V. The people disliked him so much, that they raised a rebellion, but it was soon suppressed. The Protestants were now bitterly persecuted. In the course of three years, 300 persons were burned alive, and many more were punished in other ways. Ridley and Latimer were among the first who suffered martyrdom. Hooper, Bishop of Gloucester, when tied to the stake, had the queen's pardon placed on a stool, within his reach, but he rejected it. Cranmer was next condemned. In a moment of weakness, he signed a recantation. It was no sooner done, however, than he repented, and took it back. He was immediately led to the stake. When the faggots were kindled, he stretched forth his right hand, and held it in the fire till it was consumed, saying "this hand has offended," and then, with perfect serenity, submitted to the painful martyrdom.

At the instigation of Philip, Mary made war upon France. She gained nothing by it, but lost Calais, which every king since Edward III. had regarded the chief jewel in his crown. Mary was so much grieved for the loss, that she declared that when she died, the word *Calais* would be found engraved on her heart.

When Mary first came to the throne, she was jealous of her sister, Elizabeth, and made many efforts to get rid of her. She first had her confined in the Tower, where she was very closely guarded, no one of her friends being allowed to speak to her, or even to look at her. Even a little child belonging to one of the officers of the Tower, who took pleasure in talking with her, and in bringing her flowers, was forbidden to do so, as soon as it was made known to Mary.

After being in the Tower about three months, she was removed to Woodstock, and placed under the care of Sir Henry Beddingfield, whose behaviour towards her was very harsh and insolent.

Mary then formed a plan to have Elizabeth marry the Duke of Savoy. To effect this, she sent for her to come to court, where she was treated with great kindness, feasted and flattered, but all to no purpose. She utterly refused to marry the Duke, and again left London in disgrace.

ELIZABETH.

FIFTH TUDOR.

1558.

ELIZABETH.

ELIZABETH was 25 when she came to the throne.—She was the daughter of Anne Boleyn. She was a Protestant, and England has remained so, from that time till now. The singular story of Mary, Queen of Scots, forms an interesting episode in the history of Elizabeth's reign. Mary was great niece to Henry VIII. and, as Elizabeth had once been declared illegitimate, she had some claim to the throne of England. This created a jealousy on the part of Elizabeth. Mary had been educated in France, and was a bigoted Catholic, and neither her gay manners, nor her religion were acceptable to the Scots, and she, on her part, was disgusted with the coarse manners of the people about her. Mary's character was far from virtuous, and, in 1567, she was obliged to resign her throne to her then infant son, James VI., afterwards James I. of England. Mary, soon after, threw herself into the hands of Elizabeth. She was not allowed to see Elizabeth, but imprisoned in different places. Several attempts were made by the papists, to place her on the throne, which only resulted in making her confinement more rigid and close. Elizabeth was strongly importuned by Parliament, to put her to death, but would not consent, till the most positive proofs were found that she had taken part in the conspiracy of Ballard, for the assassination of the Queen. She then, though with seemingly great reluctance, and after some months of indecision, signed the warrant for her death, an act, which she probably ever after regretted, and for which she has been severely condemned by the almost unanimous decision of the world. Mary was beheaded on the 6th February, 1587.

Cecil, Lord Burleigh, a man of great abilities, was Elizabeth's treasurer, and chief counsellor, and retained his place during his life, till near the end of her reign. Elizabeth had several proposals of marriage, but refused them all. She had several favorites, who gained great influence over her. One was Robert Dudley, Earl of Leicester—another was Ratcliffe, Earl of Sussex, and after him the Earl of Essex. Sir Walter Raleigh was also a favorite, but lost her favor entirely by marrying without her consent. Philip of Spain proposed marriage to Elizabeth, but afterwards declared war against her. His fleet, collected for this occasion, was called "The Invincible Armada." But, though deemed invincible, it was, partly by the elements, and partly by British prowess, utterly destroyed. Elizabeth's reign was long, peaceful, and prosperous. It was distinguished by the great progress of literature, and the number of eminent writers who flourished then. Among them were Spenser and Shakspeare.

The *Puritans*, a sect who were opposed to some of the forms of the Established Church, arose about this time, and Elizabeth did all she could to put them down.

JAMES I.

FIRST STUART.

1603.

JAMES I.

ELIZABETH was the last of the Tudors. Neither she, nor her sister Mary, nor her brother Edward, had any children. Elizabeth therefore appointed her cousin, James VI. of Scotland to be her successor. He was a Stuart. He was somewhat of a scholar, exceedingly pedantic and vain, and very awkward and uncouth in his manners. By him, the union of the two kingdoms was effected, though Scotland continued to have her separate Parliament till the reign of Queen Anne. A conspiracy was soon set on foot, to place Arabella Stuart on the throne. It was soon suppressed. Arabella took no part in it, and did not wish to reign; but James was jealous of her, treated her very harshly, and confined her in the Tower, where she became insane, and died.—The Catholics formed a plot, called the Gunpowder plot, to destroy the king, and the House of Lords. They employed a man, named Guy Fawkes, to execute it. They hired a vault under the House of Lords, where they placed thirty-six barrels of powder, and prepared to set fire to it, when Parliament met. But one of the conspirators, wishing to save Lord Monteagle, wrote him a letter, rather ambiguously expressed, advising him not to attend Parliament. This led to the discovery of the plot, and the execution of the conspirators.

Sir Walter Raleigh, who was engaged in the conspiracy in favor of Arabella Stuart, and had been in prison several years, under sentence of death, was liberated and sent on a voyage of discovery. Failing to find a gold mine, which he supposed existed near the Oronoco—he was beheaded on his return to England.—Lord Bacon, a distinguished philosopher, was made chancellor against the advice of Burleigh; but proving unworthy of the office, was impeached and disgraced.

It was during this reign that the present translation of the Bible was made. The manner in which this was accomplished, reflects more credit upon the character of James than perhaps any other act of his reign. Forty-seven translators were employed, selected from the most learned and able men in the kingdom, embracing, with a liberality quite unusual in those times, Puritans as well as churchmen. The rules by which they were to proceed were drawn up by the king, with great skill and prudence. They were engaged in the work about four years. The first edition was printed in 1611. As a translation it is almost, if not quite, faultless. The style is beautifully simple.

Among the worthy characters of this period, Bishops Andrews, Hooker, and Hall deserve distinguished notice.

CHARLES I.

SECOND STUART.

1625.

CHARLES I.

Charles I. was a well educated and kind hearted man, but he thought too much of his own power, and too little of the rights of the people. The Parliament was composed of many enlightened men, who had high notions of liberty. Of these, Hampden, Pym, Sir Henry Vane, and Oliver Cromwell, were among the most distinguished. On the other hand, the celebrated Sir Thomas Wentworth, afterward Lord Strafford, and Laud, Archbishop of Canterbury, were friends and supporters of the king. By their advice, Charles repeatedly dissolved Parliament, because they refused to grant the supplies he demanded. But, finding himself greatly embarrassed, and obliged to borrow money, for his necessary expenses, he was compelled to summon them again. In this way, several years were passed, in mutual vexation to the king and the Commons. In the mean time, Charles resorted to many irregular means of raising money. At length, in 1640, Strafford was impeached and condemned. Charles did all he could to save him, but was finally compelled to sign the warrant for his death. That he did so, however, was a subject of the deepest remorse, to the day of his death, and was the last thing he dwelt upon, as he stood upon the scaffold, awaiting the axe of the executioner. Laud was also impeached, but was not brought to trial till more than three years after, and was then condemned and beheaded in the seventy second year of his age.

The king's opposers were chiefly Puritans, or Round heads, as they were called. His supporters were called Cavaliers, or Malignants. These parties becoming fierce and irreconcilable, a civil war ensued, and raged six years. Charles, defeated in every quarter, finally threw himself into the hands of the Scots, who shamefully sold him to the Parliament for four hundred thousand pounds. He was imprisoned about two years, during which time many efforts were made by the Parliament, to procure his assent to a treaty which they had prepared. Charles was willing to consent to all the articles of the treaty, except two, one of which abolished Episcopacy, and the other declared that all who had taken arms in his cause were traitors. To these he would never consent. At length, Cromwell, having command of the army, violently shut out from parliament, all except the republicans. These, only about sixty in number, declared themselves "governors of the kingdom," and put an end to the treaty with the king. The king was immediately after impeached, tried before "the governors of the kingdom," and condemned. He was executed on the 20th of January, 1649.

OLIVER CROMWELL.

COMMONWEALTH.

1653.

THE COMMONWEALTH.

Though it has been said that "the king never dies"—England was now without a king. The heir to the throne, after making one daring attempt to reclaim it, from which he narrowly escaped with his life, was an exile, in poverty, and with few friends, on the continent. Parliament had been "purged," to use Cromwell's expression, and none were left to hold a seat there, but such as he chose to retain. The House of Lords was abolished. All public business was transacted in the name of *The Commonwealth*. Those who had thus succeeded in overturning the monarchy, probably desired and intended to lay the foundation of a permanent republic. But they were not themselves the right material to make it of. Bigoted, arbitrary and ambitious, they were as little disposed to allow freedom of conscience, and equal rights, to those who differed from them in opinion, as they were to submit to the unjust exactions of a royal tyrant. Nor were the people, at large, either seriously averse to a monarchy, or fully prepared to govern themselves.

Oliver Cromwell was now at the head of affairs. He first went to Ireland, as Lord Lieutenant, and then to Scotland, to reduce the "Covenanters," who refused to acknowledge the parliament. Having done this, he led his soldiers into the Hall of Parliament, drove out the members, locked the doors, and assumed to himself the reins of government, under the title of Protector. He now became, in his turn, as much of a tyrant as Charles had desired to be. In 1655, an insurrection was planned, but detected before it was ripe, and the leaders either put to death, or sold for slaves. Cormwell's government was a strong one, and much respected and feared both at home and abroad. But it was not to him a life of ease. The burden was too severe for him, and he died on the third of September, 1658, in his sixtieth year, a premature old man. His Son Richard succeeded him, but quietly resigned the place, after holding it a few months; leaving the country without any ruler, and split up into numerous factions. The old Parliament was soon assembled, the monarchy restored, and the son of the late king, who had been an exile on the Continent sixteen years, invited to the throne.

The king made many promises to conduct his government according to the laws of the realm, and to respect the rights of his subjects, who, on their part, received him with every demonstration of confidence and joy.

Richard Cromwell, though not molested by the king, left the country, and passed some time travelling on the continent under a feigned name. He lived to an advanced age, and died in the latter part of the reign of Queen Anne.

CHARLES II.

THIRD STUART.

1660.

WILLIAM AND MARY.

WILLIAM III. or William of Nassau, was grandson of Charles I., and his wife was the daughter of James II. In 1689, James, assisted by Louis XIV., made an attempt to recover the throne. The Irish, being Papists, adhered to him. He accordingly landed in Ireland with an army, which was soon increased by the accession of his friends there. He was entirely defeated in the first battle, and glad to escape again to his refuge in France, where he took upon him the severe vows of a monk, and died in 1701.

Some discontents and tumults arising among the Scots, on account of William's attempt to introduce episcopacy there, a general pardon was promised to all who would take the oath of allegiance, on a certain day. Macdonald, one of the Highland chiefs, mistaking the day, it was represented by his enemies as a wilful defiance of royal authority, and he and his clan were attacked, unarmed and unsuspicious, at Glencoe, and cruelly butchered. This excited great enmity to William, and caused him much trouble.—After this, William was much engaged in war with France, having the celebrated

Duke of Marlborough for his general. At length, a treaty of peace, called the "Peace of Ryswick," from the place where the treaty was made, was agreed upon.

Queen Mary died of small pox in 1694, and William, by a fall from his horse, in 1702.

William III. was esteemed, for his wisdom as well as his public and private virtues, as not inferior to any one who had occupied the throne since the days of Alfred. But there was a coldness and distance in his manner, which, added to the circumstance of his being a foreigner, made him somewhat unpopular in England; and more particularly so in Scotland, where, in spite of all their sufferings in their behalf, a strong interest still remained in the Stuart line of kings.

The Bank of England was established in this reign, and "the national debt" commenced.

The duke of Marlborough's family name was Churchill. He entered the army at 12 years of age, and served with consummate skill and success, during the whole of this, and the succeeding reign.

This reign was also distinguished by the writings of those great men, Locke and Dryden, and Sir Isaac Newton. The great principle of gravitation, discovered by Sir Isaac Newton, is said to have been suggested to his mind by seeing an apple fall from a tree, under which he was reading.

ANNE.

SIXTH STUART.

1702.

ANNE.

Anne, when she came to the throne, had but one child, and he died soon after, at the age of eleven. Her brother, James, was the true heir to the throne, but his claims had been set aside by the parliament, because he was a papist, and a law had been passed, settling the succession on the House of Hanover, in case Anne died without children. James was called the Pretender, and his friends Tories. The Protestant party were called Whigs. Their motto was—" We hope in God"— and the word Whig is made up of the four initials of this motto. Party spirit ran very high, and affected the ladies as well as their lords. This whole matter is finely set off, in the best vein of satire, in some admirable papers, in the Tattler and the Spectator, in which those distinguished writers, Steele and Addison, displayed their wit and talent.—War was kept up on the Continent, between England, Holland, and the Protestant states of Germany, on the one part, and France and Spain on the other, and continued till 1713, when it was terminated by the Treaty of Utrecht. During this war England gained Gibraltar.

The union of the two kingdoms was brought about in this reign, Scotland giving up her parliament, and sending forty-five Commoners, and sixteen Peers to the English parliament.

There were many distinguished writers at this time in England—among whom Pope, Steele, Addison, and Swift were very conspicuous.

Queen Anne, as has been stated before, was married to Prince George of Denmark. She was very desirous that he should be proclaimed king. To this, however, the parliament would not consent. George was, by no means, ambitious, either of the title or the power, but was content, like Prince Albert, at the present time, to be the first subject of the crown. Prince George died in 1709. His death was a severe blow to the queen, who was devotedly attached to him.

Anne had some misgivings, it is said, about wearing the crown, her father having forbidden her to do so, as it would be standing in the way of her brother's rights, whom the parliament had illegally set aside from the succession. She had a secret interview with her brother, whom she was much disposed to favor, but was unable to do any thing for him. She died August 5, 1714.

GEORGE I.

FIRST GUELPH.

1714.

GEORGE I.

ALTHOUGH Anne is generally called the last of the Stuarts, George had no real claim to the throne except as a Stuart. He was great grandson to James 1. But, as his father was a prince in his own country, he and his descendants have retained the family name. The king favored the Whigs, with Sir Robert Walpole, as minister. Party spirit ran very high.

The Earl of Mar raised the standard of James Stuart, "the Pretender," in Scotland. Jan. 16, 1716, was fixed for his coronation, but before that day arrived he was defeated by the Duke of Argyle, and driven back to France.

The great "South Sea Bubble" occupied the attention, and ruined the fortunes of many people at this time. It was a scheme contrived by Sir John Blunt, to concentrate all the national debts into one fund, by which it was supposed they would be much enhanced in value, and so an immense profit accrue to the purchasers. It terminated, like most other speculations, in a ruinous loss to all concerned.

The death of George I. was very sudden. He had left England, on a visit to Hanover, on the 3d of June, 1777, but was taken ill on the journey. He was so anxious to reach his brother's castle, that he could not be prevailed upon to stop; and he died in his carriage, on the 10th of the month, just before reaching Osnaburg.

His unfortunate wife had died just seven months before him. Her name was Sophia of Zell. She was confined, no less than 32 years, in a castle of her husband's, innocent, as was generally believed, of any crime; though George might, and probably *did* believe her unworthy of his affection. Her son, George the Second, was firmly persuaded of her innocence; but he was never allowed to see her, though he once went to the castle where she was confined, for that purpose. His wife, also, the future Queen Caroline, believed her to be an injured and guiltless woman.

Whether it were so or not, no one can hear of her long confinement, and of her earnest protestations of innocence, knowing at the same time that she had no fair trial, without feeling the strongest indignation at the cruelty and tyranny of her husband; especially when it is considered that his own character was by no means free from reproach.

George II. was much more beloved by the English people than George I., even during the life of the latter, which caused no little jealousy between the father and son. This unhappy feeling was so nurtured and increased, by the mischievous interference of the busy bodies about the court, that it terminated in an out-right quarrel.

GEORGE II.

SECOND GUELPH.

1727.

GEORGE II.

GEORGE II., though more acceptable to the English than his father, was still too much of a German to suit them altogether. His Scotch subjects did not like him at all, and were soon engaged in another effort to place "the Pretender," James Stuart, on the throne.

George had entered into the war, in which nearly all Europe was involved, to sustain Maria Theresa, daughter of Charles VI., in her claim to the imperial throne, which was disputed by the Elector of Bavaria. Advantage was taken of this absence of the king and his army, to invade England. Charles Edward, the eldest son of "the Pretender," made one attempt in 1744, with 15,000 men, aided by the king of France. This proving unsuccessful, he made a second attempt, and a more formidable one, the following year. He landed at Borodale, in Scotland, and was joined by numbers of the Highlanders. All England was thrown into commotion. The king was sent for to return immediately. Thirty thousand pounds were offered for the person of Charles Stuart, who, in his turn, offered the same sum for the king. The prince advanced to Perth, where he proclaimed his father king, and then took possession of Edinburgh. He soon after gained a considerable victory over the king's forces, which secured to him the greater part of Scotland. Then, invading England, penetrated to within four days' march of London, but was obliged to retreat, and was at length, totally defeated on the field of Culloden, in April, 1746. Thus ended the last effort in favor of the Stuarts. Notwithstanding the large reward offered for his arrest, Charles contrived to escape. The poor Highlanders concealed him several months, often at the risk of their own lives. Some of his escapes are almost too wonderful for sober history. The cruelties inflicted upon his adherents, are disgraceful to all who were concerned, especially to the Duke of Cumberland, who commanded the king's forces.

The English were now constantly engaged in wars, on the Continent, and in America. Canada was taken from the French, not without the loss of General Wolfe, one of the greatest of English commanders. Mr. Pitt, the celebrated Earl of Chatham, was now at the head of affairs, and the English were almost every where successful.

The names of Anson, Hawke, and Boscawen are distinguished in the naval history of this reign.

Sir Robert Walpole, Sir William Pulteney, Mr. Pelham, the Duke of New Castle, and Mr. Pitt, were successively leaders of the administration.

GEORGE III

THIRD GUELPH.

1760.

GEORGE III.

George III. was a quiet, religious man, kind and charitable to all. His reign was so long, busy, and eventful, it is impossible to more than hint at some of the principal events. One of the most remarkable was the American Revolution, by which, for the sake of proudly carrying out a system of unjust and unequal taxation, England lost the fairest and best of her foreign colonies. It is but just to say that some of her most distinguished men, among whom Pitt was foremost, strenuously opposed the policy of the crown to the last. This celebrated statesman, died, as it were, with the words of remonstrance on his lips. In the midst of an eloquent speech, in the House of Lords, he fell back in convulsions, and died a few days after.

The French Revolution, also, and the wonderful achievements of Napoleon Buonaparte, from his origin, as an obscure Corsican, through all his proud and brilliant career, to his defeat at Waterloo, and his confinement, first at Elba, and then at St. Helena, belong to this period. Lord Nelson, Mr. Fox, the younger Pitt, Mr. Percival, Lord Exmouth, Sir John Moore, the Duke of Wellington, and many other distinguished men, bore conspicuous parts in the conduct of public affairs. This period is equally distinguished by great names in the various departments of literature, science, and philanthropy, and by those great engines of benevolence, missionary, and Bible, and kindred associations, and by the abolition of the slave trade. The king was insane during the last ten years of his reign, and his son, the Prince of Wales, was Regent.

There were many changes of administration during the long reign of George III. Lord Chatham, the Duke of New Castle, Lord Bute, Mr. George Grenville, the Marquis of Rockingham, the Duke of Grafton, Lord North, Mr. Fox, and Lord Shelburne, successively occupied the Premiership, previous to 1783. The younger Pitt, second son of Lord Chatham, then held it until 1801, when he resigned. He was succeeded by the Duke of Portland, and Mr. Addington, afterwards Viscount Sidmouth. Mr. Pitt came in again in 1804. He died in 1806, and was succeeded by his great rival, Mr. Fox, who also died before the close of the year. Next came Mr. Percival, who was retained in office until 1812, when he was assassinated, in the lobby of the house of commons, by a Mr. Bellingham, in revenge, as he said, for a private injury, which he had received at the hands of the government.

This reign was longer, by four years, than any other in the English annals—and was as marked by important events as by its length.

GEORGE IV.

FOURTH GUELPH.

1820.

GEORGE IV.

GEORGE IV., as has been stated, exercised all the functions of royalty, as Regent, during the last ten years of his father's life. Whatever might have been his advantages of education, in an intellectual point of view, his moral and religious education had been entirely neglected. His character was that of a profligate, from his youth up. Accordingly he never possessed the respect or the affection of his people.

He married his cousin, Caroline of Brunswick. He never loved her; and, as might be expected from one of his character, never treated her well. Their only child was the Princess Charlotte, who seems to have adorned her elevated station by a character combining all that was attractive and lovely in woman. She was married to Leopold, then Prince of Saxe Coburg, and now King of Belgium, but died, lamented by the whole nation, about a year after her marriage.

The disaffection between George IV. and Queen Caroline, had gone so far that they had been, for many years, separated from each other. On his accession to the throne, he brought her to a public trial before the House of Lords, on a charge of the most abandoned wickedness. These charges were not proved, and she soon after died, protesting her innocence.

The king's conduct in this case disgusted and incensed the people, who thought that in view of his own abandoned character, he should have been the last to bring such a charge against his wife. The excitement was so great, that a desperate contest took place at the time of her funeral; the people, at the cost of some blood, compelling the procession to pass through London.

The great act of catholic emancipation, by which Roman Catholics became entitled to hold seats in Parliament, and offices under government, belongs to this reign. The whole world was now at peace, and commerce and the arts flourished every where.

The latter years of George's life were passed in retirement, chiefly at a secluded cottage in Windsor Park. He seldom met with his Parliament in person, or showed himself to the people in any public place. He died in the summer of 1830—received a splendid burial—but was neither honored nor lamented by his people.

It is neither title, nor power, nor a life of luxury, nor a magnificent burial, nor a splendid mausoleum, that constitutes a claim upon the respect or regard of the world. The king, and the hero, as well as the private citizen, must respect the laws of God and man, if they would secure an honorable or grateful remembrance in the hearts of men.

WILLIAM IV.

FIFTH GUELPH.

1830.

WILLIAM IV.

The Duke of Clarence, the third son of George III. succeeded, as William IV. He had been a valuable officer in the navy, and was popular with the people. As a king, he favored every project for reform. Among others, the abolition of slavery in the colonies, an object long sought for by British philanthropists, was now accomplished. Sir Robert Peel, Lord Brougham, the Duke of Wellington, and many other great names, who took part in the affairs of this reign, still survive.

The country was prosperous at home and abroad; manufactures, agriculture and commerce, engrossed the attention of the people. Literature and science made constant advances; and, but for the extreme poverty of the great mass of the labouring classes, England might be looked upon as one of the most favored countries on the face of the earth. For although her government is a monarchy, her people are as free, and as fully protected in all their rights, as those of any nation on earth.

But with all her freedom, and glory, and wealth, there is one side of the picture that is fearfully dark and portentous. The long and expensive wars, which have given to her arms so much renown, and added so largely to her territories in every quarter of the globe, have created a burden of debt under which the very island seems to groan. The enormous expenses of government, the host of pensioned favorites and dependants, and the immense sums necessary to pay only the interest on her public debt, make it necessary to impose burdensome and almost insupportable taxes upon the people. There is no article of necessity or comfort that does not feel this oppressive burden. The light of heaven, and the very air they breathe, are taxed. And though there is, perhaps, more wealth and splendor among the nobility of England, than is to be found any where else under heaven, there is also more abject poverty, more absolute, hopeless misery and starvation, among the lowest classes, particularly in the manufacturing districts, and in the mines, than is known in any other country on earth. Such a state of things cannot long exist among a people, whose history is the history of freedom struggling with oppression, and right overcoming might.

It is earnestly to be hoped that the revolution which *must* take place, sooner or later, will be a peaceful and bloodless one—that some sagacious and far-seeing statesman will arise, and provide a remedy for evils which, if not soon removed, must inevitably overwhelm in ruin one of the fairest portions of the globe.

VICTORIA.

SIXTH GUELPH.

1837.

VICTORIA.

VICTORIA, the only child of the Duke of Kent, who was the fourth son of George III. came to the throne in 1837, at the age of eighteen. She was soon after married to Prince Albert of Saxe Coburg, brother to King Leopold of Belgium.

The Queen was desirous to have her husband invested with the dignity and prerogatives of royalty, but to this the parliament would not consent. He, therefore, stands, as did Philip, during Mary's reign, and George, during that of Anne, the first subject of the crown. In case, however, of the death of the Queen, before her son, the young Prince of Wales, arrives at majority, Prince Albert will act as Regent.

The principal events of the present reign are, the war upon China, and the repeal agitation of Ireland, under the great leader, O'Connell.—The object of O'Connell is, that Ireland shall have a separate parliament, to be held in Dublin, as was the case till the year 1800. It was also the case in Scotland till the reign of Queen Anne. This agitation rose so high in the year 1843, that O'Connell and some of his party were impeached of treason, tried, convicted, and imprisoned. They have since been set at liberty, the House of Lords having reversed the judgment of the court, and the repeal agitation is still going on, though not quite as bravely as before.

The war in China, though one of the most unjust and oppressive that ever disgraced the escutcheon of a Christian nation, will probably result in great good to China, and the world. That great nation, comprising about one-third part of the population of the globe, has hitherto been almost entirely shut out from intercourse with other nations. Her doors are now thrown open to such an extent, that there is little reason to doubt, that Christian missionaries will find their way into all parts of the empire. And, as almost the whole population can read, they will be accessible at once through the press. The government has already made very favorable treaties with England and the United States, and another is in progress with France.

One of the interesting incidents of Victoria's peaceful reign, is the interchange of royal visits with the crowned heads of the continent. A few years ago, a king or emperor could hardly go from one palace to another, in his own dominions, without a small army to protect his life. Now, they travel without fear or molestation, wherever they choose; and make neighborly visits, and morning calls, like other people. This is the legitimate fruit of peace, now of 30 years' continuance.

REGAL SUCCESSION.

The following lines may serve to assist the memory in retaining the order of succession. Something of the same kind appeared several years ago, in one of the New York papers, but, though diligently sought for, we have not been able to find it.

> From the end of the Heptarchy down to this date,
> There are fifty-six monarchs, and dynasties eight;
> First fifteen were Saxons, and then came the Dane,
> Of these there were three, then two Saxons again.
> The conquering Normans count only four,
>   The Plantagenets fourteen,
> Five Tudors, six Stuarts, and now of the Guelphs,
>   The sixth is Victoria the queen.

> The conquering Normans were only four.
> Two Williams, a Henry, and Stephen—no more;
> Then the fourteen Plantagenets came on,—
> From Henry the second, through Richard and John,
> Third Henry, three Edwards, and Richard the vain,
> Three Henrys, two Edwards, to Richard again;
> The Tudors were five—two Henrys, young Ned,
> Bloody Mary, and Bessy the royal old maid;
> The Stuarts were six—first James, as you've seen,
> And then the two Charleses, with Cromwell between,
> James second, and William, and Anne the queen;
> Of the Guelphs, four Georges and William are past,
> And long may Victoria be the last.

NOTE.

By reference to the list of Kings belonging to the period of "EARLY HISTORY," it will be perceived that the number is less by two, than we have given in the "REGAL SUCCESSION," on the last page. The discrepancy occurs in this way. *Ethalbald* and *Ethelbert*, brothers of *Alfred*, reigned by usurpation, their father having not only appointed *Alfred* his successor, but procured him to be anointed by the Pope. They also reigned at the same time, over different portions of the Kingdom, and not over the whole. They were, therefore, not regarded as properly Kings of England; while Ethelred, another brother, who reigned after them, during the minority of Alfred, is admitted into the list, because he possessed an undivided throne.

In the "REGAL SUCCESSION," the full number is restored, in order to accommodate it to Professor Gouraud's system, which has now become familiar to so many, that any deviation from it would be only making confusion, without promising any advantage to counterbalance it.

JOSIAH ADAMS,

BRICK CHURCH CHAPEL,

OPPOSITE THE CITY HALL,

NEW YORK.

PUBLISHER OF THE FOLLOWING POPULAR GAMES:

THE GAME OF KINGS.

From the Salem Gazette of January 28.

THE GAME OF KINGS,—*New York*—JOSIAH ADAMS. This is one of the most interesting games we have ever seen offered for the entertainment and instruction of children. It is an arrangement of the Kings of England, from the Conquest to the present time, in a series of cards, thirty-six in number; each card has a handsome representation of a monarch, with the date of his ascent to the throne, and the prominent events and names suggested by his reign, furnishing questions by which the players can test each other's familiarity with these points of history. Every one who can answer the questions suggested by the card he holds in his hand, is entitled to keep it, and at the end of the game he is the winner who holds the greatest number of cards. Parents and children can play together at this game with pleasure and profit; and the elders would do well to rub up their acquaintance with dates and matters of history, lest the well taught youths of the present day, who have so many railroads to learning, should beat them. This attractive game which we would recommend to every family circle, is for sale at the book store of *Francis Putnam.*

PORTLAND, (Me.) January 16, 1845.

Mr. JOSIAH ADAMS, New York.

Sir—Allow me to say to you that I look upon the "Game of Kings," of which I am told you are the publisher, as one of the best contrived, and most provident helps I know of, not only for children, but for *all*, in the study of English History. No man alive can be sure of himself upon any subject, till he is called upon to teach. What we think we are most familiar with, may fail us at a pinch, if we are not obliged to make use of it in the daily business of life.

By this beautiful and modest contrivance, children are made at one and the same time, both learners and teachers; and better still. self-teachers,—and if they who are no longer children—nay, if their fathers and mothers are not too old nor too busy to learn, the sooner they join the class with their babies, the better will it be for both.

It would soon satisfy them how little they know of the great *Game of Kings*—the *World's History*—and how easy it may be for the oldest and the busiest to know all that is worth knowing of both. In a word, sir, I congratulate you and the contriver, on the simplicity and beauty of his invention. I take it for granted he is a father, and hope you are, otherwise you would not be likely to understand the whole importance of such help—and wish you both all the success you so richly deserve.

Yours and his, whoever he (or she) may be, with many thanks for your contribution to the great first cause on earth, *Education.*

JOHN NEAL.

From the New York Evening Mirror.

ACQUISITION OF ENGLISH HISTORY MADE AN AMUSEMENT.—The "Game of Kings," a most ingenious and fascinating contrivance for children, was the New Year's Present which we believe *stayed as a classic*, when the holidays and their ephemerals went by. It is still for sale by Adams, Brick Church book store.

From the (Portland) Christian Mirror, January 30.

THE GAME OF THE KINGS.—We have seen a " pack of cards," which we can very conscientiously introduce to our young readers, and which we are willing their parents, and older friends should join them in using. They compose a brief history of the English monarchs from the Conquest to the present time, with an engraved likeness of each. At the top are placed —the number of the reign from 1 to 36—the name of the monarch—the family name, and number of the family—the date at which his reign commenced on the left, and the length of the reign on the right; at the bottom, prominent events, distinguished men, and metrical lines or verses recognizing some important event in the reign. A supernumerary card gives directions for conducting the play, or profitably using the collection; and another gives a list of the Saxon and Danish Kings, with the date and duration of their reigns, previous to the Conquest. Moreover with the cards, is furnished a neat little book of sixteen pages, giving in short, condensed forms, a biography of each of the thirty-six kings, with the most noticeable events and characters of the reign of each. The child who will fix in the memory the facts, rendered available by this ingenious device—and almost any one will readily do it, with a companion or two to co-operate—will have at command more of English history, than some adults who have devoted months to mere reading. The use of it will waken attention—quicken and strengthen the power of recollection, and furnish profitable and pleasant employment for many an hour, which might otherwise hang heavily, or be sadly misspent. The Cards may be had of Joseph S. Bailey, Exchange Building, in styles of various elegance, and at different prices. We trust the inventor will extend his plan, and if it be not too soon, will yet give us " The Game of the Republic."

THE NEW WORLD,

A GAME OF AMERICAN HISTORY.

BY A YANKEE.

This new game, which is beautifully got up, is caculated to be more popular than any other in this country. It comprises a brief history of the Discovery, Colonization and Progress of this Country, distributed into sixteen cards, with appropriate embellishments, accompanied with sixteen cards of questions, and a book of explanation—and will be afforded at a very low price.

THE ERRAND BOY

OR

JACK AT ALL TRADES.

A Game of Mechanical Trades.

This game is designed for the amusement of very young children; though, at the same time that it amuses, it also instructs them in relation to several of the most important articles in common use—the sources whence they are obtained, the manner in which they are produced. It cannot fail to interest the young, as the game itself is of an active and exciting character, while the information it affords, is conveyed in an amusing manner.

89096180112

b89096180112a

Lightning Source UK Ltd.
Milton Keynes UK
UKHW020934041022
409903UK00007B/550